THIS FESTIVAL OF LEAVES

Poems

Jim Glaser

ACKNOWLEDGEMENTS

ISBN 978-0-692-80518-3 (paperback)
Library of Congress Control Number: 2016919269

The poems listed below were first published in the periodicals mentioned: "In Spring," *The Christian Century*; "The Most Beautiful Day of the Year," *The Pasadena Star News*; "Balzac," *The Christian Science Monitor*; "Summer Rain," and "The Toast," *Samsara Magazine*; "The Hawk," *The Hook*; "Shhhhh!" and "Sky Sailor," *Spring*; Some of the shorter poems were published in *Hummingbird Magazine.*

Cover design by Art Bookbindery, Canada
Printed and bound in Canada by Art Bookbindery

First printing: 2016
Publisher: Jim Glaser
523 N. Midland Ave., Nyack, New York, USA, 10960
email: jamesglaser1@yahoo.com

"The unanswerable question has always
an answer in compassion"

-- Lin Yutang

These poems are dedicated to my family and
friends –friends in California, friends in
New York, friends in the Midwest, and especially
to my daughters Tana and Shannon, and my partner, Diane.

They are also dedicated to my friends in the
Whittier Writers' Club—Poetry Section who were
my mentors for many years and to the Nyack Poets'
Circle for their ongoing comradeship. Special
thanks to my friend Ernest Sherman, poet, for his
careful reading of this manuscript. Without the
support and helpful advice of my artist-partner,
Diane Churchill, and my family, this collection would
not have been possible.

TABLE OF CONTENTS

Preface

I

WINDOWS

Window / 2

As a woman... / 4

Hutch's restaurant ... / 5

Sometimes I think... / 8

My birthright... / 9

Cabin / 10

Stationery / 11

Rock From a Santa Barbara Beach / 12

Weight / 13

Of the Earth / 14

Sometimes I Envy Stone / 16

"Ugly" / 17

The Measurers / 18

Ghosts /19

Is That What Kafka Meant / 20

I missed… / 22

II

SOUNDINGS

This Spring / 24

Still Life / 25

You There! / 26

Soundings / 27

freedom… / 28

I hold two dreams… / 29

The Survivor / 30

The Tightrope Walker… / 31

For the New Year / 33

Hunger / 34

mother of being… / 35

1975 / 36

A Note From Ryokan / 39

Garden Wall / 40

silence is a pond… / 41

III

THE CIRCUS

Shhh! / 44

The Clown / 45

Blindness / 47

Relay Race / 49

A Note From Huck Finn / 51

From the Diary of Le / 52

Playing Banjo on the Corner... / 54

The Myth of "We-as-a-Child" / 55

Metro North / 57

Evening of Outdoor Jazz / 58

A Season of Words / 59

River / 60

magnolia most voluptuous... / 62

The Limp / 63

Coffee cup / 65

IV

THE RIVER

a poem can be... / 68

Balzac / 69

a poem is a way... / 70

The River / 71

You Will Know / 72

Prometheus / 73

Snow Walk / 74

poem written on the back... / 75

Odysseus to His Daughter / 76

this emptiness... / 78

This Hawk / 79

Just Before / 81

Yes and No / 82

Late afternoon... / 83

jacaranda... / 84

just outside... / 85

Red / 86

Transformation / 87
House of whispers... / 88

V

AFTER RAIN

In Spring / 92
Summer Rain / 93
The Cry / 95
After Rain / 96
The Most Beautiful Day... / 97
Wintergarden / 98
After Visiting My Mother ... / 99
leave room for fear... / 100
Epiphany / 101
For a Friend ... / 102
"Just like Phil " / 103
you see... / 104
Sad and Gentle Giant / 105
Presidential Election... /107

John Brown's Farm /108

Net of Tears / 109

Reduced to Stone / 111

like some blind fruit... / 123

For Edward / 124

This Knowledge / 125

VI

SHARECROPPING

I move in music... / 128

Huntington Library: Beside the Pond / 129

Alley Walk / 130

Launch / 132

Sharecropping / 133

Standing Figure--Knife Edge / 135

Communion / 136

The Hawk / 137

Cold Walk / 138

Alba Plena / 140

scattered in sun... / 142

Sky Sailor / 143

Flying Bridge / 144

Cicadas In the Morning.../ 145

Two Chinese Poems / 146

Sailing Off Redondo Beach / 148

VII

BLUE

A Note to Odysseus /150

walk before dawn... / 151

The wind ... / 152

The Stranger / 153

Sweet Clover / 154

spring light rain... / 155

a stillness comes... / 156

There never was more... / 157

With Love / 158

morning after rain... / 159

presence is a country… / 160
I Have Come / 161
Dawn Girl / 162
morning you walk by… / 163
I Seem to Hear Small Bells / 164
Lying holding each other… / 165
Blue / 166
Cascading Time / 167
"Eros" / 169
On the Way / 170
All the Words / 171
Silhouette / 173

PREFACE

TO MY NOTEBOOKS

Most of them
          are gone now
thrown away
-- they never were
          for others eyes
They were not a record of my days

Scrawled   redundant incoherent
written on the run
one gigantic word   a line in the dark
with chalk with markers
stained   torn
more like "letters from the front"
          -- at least my "front"
a way of tunneling through
  crawling over   finding my way
     on hopeless ground
a way of hanging on
          stunned turned upside down
    shaken by the real -- that wind that face that hand

As a potter   suddenly
      jumping from his stool
   grabbing a lump of clay
    and yelling "YES!"
-- my notebooks and their poems

were the hands
        the lump of clay
    my YES!

I

WINDOWS

WINDOW

It sits there in front of my eyes like a dirty window
I am looking through *now*
  at *then*
or like a foggy view   or only a partial one
-- my first memory of a day --
and I find myself standing at the
front door of the house
and outside is the field
right next door to the left
a huge vacant field
no trees or one far off   grass taller than we are

I see myself out there   a ways off
in the field and Judy is with me   Judy and our dog
we're pushing our way through the forest of weeds
Davie is on ahead somewhere out of sight
the place is so wild and brambly that we aren't
making good time
the sky   it's kind of cloudy
maybe it's late in the afternoon
we are looking for berries
we're playing with the dog   we're running together
it's a little chilly   I think it's early fall

that sky that grass the air
that day -- it's like it was one never ending day

In the beginning was the house
we called it the "old cold house" and I think we were cold but I think that was my Mom's name for it
My Mom there is like a warm cloud all around kind of always in the background
My Father is moving so fast that I can't really see him...he is going up the stairs to the attic...there are strange things up there
-- big model planes I think -- gliders that he made

There is no school for me or for Davie or Judy
no city only one or two other houses
the field our steps our house
us wandering half awake to things
that's all

*

As a woman waits
for the child in her to be born
I wait
for that which is being born in me

Longing
ripples from me
and breaking
fingers the shore

HUTCH'S RESTAURANT AT NIGHT

In a dark wooden frame
on one wall
there's the picture
I remember from my grandmother's house
of Jesus as a boy
          the simple face   the long dark hair
   the white tunic

Looking at him tonight
it's suddenly summer
and I'm a boy again
visiting the small town with strange sidewalks
and huge maple trees that always seem to be
looking down on me and saying,
     "So, it's you again!"
and there's the sugar-beet factory
behind the house   across the field
     and three children who've never done it before
are discovering potatoes in the mounds in
     grandmother's garden

Now its Sunday
There's laughter from the "summer house"
that is really a picnic table enclosed in screen
-- the large family
 is eating sweet corn out there on Sunday
and grandmother with her apron on

comes out of the kitchen
carrying a pie
only to disappear again
and she's short and chubby
-- her hair is in braids rolled up on her head
and she's smiling silently
and my head comes just at the huge pillow
of her breasts

We walk to the bank in the morning
and the moment they see us
walk through the door
they usher us right into the office
and grandpa
        rises up so tall and elegant with that smile
and saying "Well, well!" with that softness in
his eyes

And evening comes to a close
in yellow lamp-light
and I go slowly up the dark wooden
staircase past the crowd of friendly faces
on the stairwell wall -- all of them knowing
these soft steps and this not unfriendly darkness
and I know the strange bed loaned to me
for a week each summer in the odd room
and I lie awake long
immersed in the scent of someone else's life as
a hidden part of my own

and my father's breath and his brothers'
whisper with mine

*

Sometimes I think you
really don't know
you have a
way

That you really think you have
no destiny
of your own
because no one tells you
about it
because all it offers you
is your very own
life

*

My birthright
is a
single
slender
stalk
of actuality
a shadow pressing on a stone

CABIN

I have my own place to stay
in this wilderness -- a home within
my larger home -- full of cracks

Hell if I had wanted a refuge
I never would have come at all

WINDOW

Your rippled picture of the world
is not enough

Between the summer wind
and me
your loose panes will never last

STATIONERY

It had a picture of a wild looking
boy
      hair long and straggly
      bare to the waist
      below that an animal skin

He was sitting on a large rock
blowing on a curved animal horn into
a hazy brown sky

I wanted it
            not to write on
but to be

ROCK FROM A SANTA BARBARA BEACH

Perhaps the hands that held him
          dropped away
and he
          like some great ship
          bowing to its stars
slipped into chaos
                              clung
to his sucking tomb
          like some sailor in `a storm
          clinging to a rail

and his blood
in heaving   dark
                              prenatal swells
swept all the way to his fingertips

Immersed in darkness
          surging for the shore
perhaps his almost bursting fingers
first found you
          the knob
on some great door

WEIGHT

I have tried to shift this
heavy stone
from one hand to the other
I have tried to lay this growth
at your feet
I have wet my palms in cool water
and have waited for the wind
to evaporate the ache

But tonight
I feel it hiding somewhere close
at hand
its long thin fingers stretched far out
wide as all pain

I hear it cry and
I want to ask its name

OF THE EARTH

Perhaps we use grief
as trees use sleep the long night
of winter

the slow sap thickens
and the depleted eye turns inward
and some darker gentler sun rises
from the earth
and the hand is slow enough and wise
to harvest fragments
of lost light

How would so changed a thing
receive the touch of light and wind
warmth and rain
again

**

The outside light and air
could not penetrate
Grandma Beckett's house
Its dusty air was heavy with
legends of brave men and their boats
and of old Great Grandmother
rocking at the window
waiting for them

Their faces their dark and massive furniture
had claimed the place
and when -- come summer -- we came
again to visit
surrounded my slim life as well
with something deep and old
benevolent as earth

One visit older by myself
just Grandma there then
I slept in your old room mother

Your high school picture on the dresser
and my first poem
Some weave of time and love
some glance from you
mingled with the calling
of the earth

SOMETIMES I ENVY STONE

Today my shadow
          strikes the ground
with too much force

the clearest things I see
are those few trees that stand
          completely still
everything that quivers
          hiding

Why are they allowed to go
          unnoticed as the stones
while the quickly passing nun
          spies me

"UGLY"

They laughed
and gave it to her
for a
            name

It
tore through her own
-- not the paper thin rag she wore
but the skin

THE MEASURERS

They stood him up
against a golden tower
  They found him small

They should have matched
his eyes
against the morning
        or a star

GHOSTS

As you move smugly
off the field
reassured of your potency with me
I fling this inaudible whisper
at your cool uncovered heels:

I may be terrified of you
but tonight at least
I am not
guilty

IS THAT WHAT KAFKA MEANT

Now
I
know
what these idiosyncrasies
mean:
my masters
Buber
Hesse
and Fromm
have stretched me well
each in his own direction

With genuine affection I bow
and strike off
alone

What if I stopped
trying to twist these wriggling threads
into a single rope?
What if this land is fertile
and that's why it dreams such restless
dreams?

Suddenly silent inside
I stand
directly on the road--
kicked out
nothing more said

no wound up spring inside
no certain where to go

a silent candle burning slow   then
a trickle of fantasy:
"What if I could keep from running
back and learn to say (like Kafka?)
'It's kind of funny
but
it's me'
-- I'll bet it could be fun here!"

*

I

missed

much

of you

II

SOUNDINGS

THIS SPRING

I want my life
that no one has stolen
        that has slipped away
that has been absorbed by the ground
        that has been driven away
by the wind
and baked dry by the sun
that has been carried off at night by
strange animals
        that has drowned silently and alone

Spring -- ghost of my life
        haunts this land
and will not rest
                will not let me rest
My spring -- demands to speak within all voices
works its way in through all cracks
in all doors
        threads its way into all weaves
weaves its way back into the fabric
of my bones

My spring -- ache in the muscles of my hand
        my spring -- cry in the back of my
throat
        "Alive! All of me!"

STILL LIFE

the plant on the glass table
has pale green leaves that curve
and curl
one looks like a fairy slipper
and one
holds itself high
its full surface facing me frankly
the light on it speaking like skin

YOU, THERE

How did you get in?
And how have you remained a shadow with
such darkness as today
striking you in the face? Nothing but a wish
of cobwebs and a shim of dust how has your
meandering form escaped the whip of winter
that has lashed our flesh all day --
          but here you are at dusk!
And what is that slow dance in mimic of?

"The way the willows sway in spring" you say

               You are a dream

"And more" you say
               "I am what is left --
what still remains of that sweet innocence
that was your skin
what has survived the war with that huge bird
who hovered here and took the name of god
and claimed you for a sacrifice
I am the passion fear could not at last
control
the love that did not die when love
was trampled down by death
I am the unextinguished flame that dances
at the core"

SOUNDINGS

Large
beneath the surface
always shifting out of the light
protected
                    from words
hunger
huge
known only by my body
     like another kind of being

You are the one who moves
rhythmically in me
in the darkness
touching
knowing this place differently

-- Come into the light!
Bring all that you have --
I need you

*

Freedom

-- silence standing
at

an open door

*

I hold two dreams
                    inviolate

      one that
fights its way to the surface
and finally bubbles from my lips

and
      one that comes
small and barefoot
sits beside me silently
and calls my name
            until I hear

THE SURVIVOR

We had not heard his cries had thought
him lost had shut the hatches just
before the storm

Next morning when we
found him he was clinging to a rail
That tight embrace of welded skin and iron
had saved him but we could not coax him and
we would not pry him loose

All day we waited for his glassy look
to fade -- it did not nor did he speak
And when he slept his fingers as they
slipped jerked awake and grasped convulsively

Ship's doctor and friend I stayed with him
throughout that night
Towards morning he
slowly let his fingers loosen   then let go
and slept.
But the chaos never left his hands

Sometimes I see them tremble   but I never
ask him more

THE TIGHTROPE WALKER--TO HIS PARTNER
(ON HIS BACK)

I hear you Little--
you don't want me to take the first step --
you want me to stay here
on the platform
and think about it
and think
and think   and think -- or maybe
to go back down
You know we'd only find ourselves up
here again--remember?
You know this is where we belong

Yes I do understand -- you are afraid
Of course I care about that
I care about you!
And I'm with you
But look   there is nothing more we need to
think about
Little we need a different kind of "thinking" now
to make it
we need to be very sensitive to this
rope beneath my feet --
we need to sense its every movement together
as if it were a voice -- a signal
we need to pick up signals of both kinds --
from the rope
and from ourselves and adjust

our balance and our speed ever so slightly

Of course I'll talk to you -- all along the way
we're a team aren't we?

FOR THE NEW YEAR

What if
this longing is really the scent
of something hidden in the crisp
present

what if this fear
points like a quivering finger
to something struggling to be born
at the center

and what if
breathing is the beginning of love
and even the smallest movement
readies us
to receive a world

HUNGER
(a vision)

She stood right in front of me
reached out
and held my hand

"You look desperate and confused
like a man who is starving
Perhaps I know something of this hunger
Perhaps I know something of what you hope for

"Put your hand in mine for a moment
Feel me weaving one part of you with another
Feel! that is your hunger
Touch!

Feel me drawing you into all of your life
from the inside"

*

mother of being
sea of my birth and my always beginning
your thick breath
flows in my mouth

your warm seas
breathe in my bones

1975

This is how it was
as best I can say
-- maybe someday I will
be able to say it better
or simpler

It was about 40 years
ago
sitting in my room
broad daylight
late afternoon
summer alone
my family away on vacation

I can't tell you what I was thinking about
but a gloom like a heavy blanket
fell over me
like it used to do
as a child --- at night
and later as a seminary student
at any time
a starless heavy night
a cold hopeless
aloneness going on
forever -- infinite

I cringed inside
as I had always done under
its spell

This time
I saw something else
I held on to something else
something
happened
and it happened at that one moment
and it happened again and again over time

All I can say is this:
like a whoosh from somewhere
blowing into that night
like a strong warm wind
like a hand

A word
from somewhere came
A word thick clear unspoken:
the word "intimate"
sweeping away that blanket
of despair
A word for a lifetime

I can't explain it
and how all that day and for some days afterwards
I was in a daze
something in me
pointing to *this everything* given -- to me here
this silent flower…*this* cloud streaming sky…
this sunlit tree trunk…*these* people on the bus
each "thing" with its own new brightness

Something flowing between us all
…nothing separate
something within me flowing
with everything

I didn't see this in my mind's eye
I felt-saw it all at once -- how can I say it?
…people individual people young and old…
stretching out each in their lives I saw them
I felt them reaching me
I was among them -- and reaching for them
for all of this
and yet nothing was separate
everything was connected -- for me to reach…
to know…to laugh with …to love in some way unknown

And I had to scribble wherever whenever however
-- a kind of music a dance a way of listening expressing
the life in me that had started up

Everything was more vivid than my fear

For the first time
I knew I was part of everything

In this embrace
was and remains my embracing

A NOTE FROM RYOKAN

(for L.M.)

Gamble this my friend
-- rely on your heart

Take your stand here
in wind in rain in sun
-- arms outstretched

Your love comes in silence
out of the emptiness

GARDEN WALL

I love your gray
          contented face
your cheek always
          against the wind
your frank and simple boldness
touching shoulders
with the sun

*

silence is a pond
      one tremulous reedy call
again
              and   again

carried across the long stretch
      of perfectly still water

III

THE CIRCUS

SHHHHHH!

(It's a secret:

You

and all the world

are

magical

        ((almost

almost

      almost overwhelmingly so))

)

THE CLOWN

An empty football field tonight
instead of a sawdust ring --
the children in bleachers
instead of huddled together
in the palm of a big tent

It's the tents I miss the most
I'm not talking
about shelters from the sun or rain
for one or two day stands -- like now --
but huge flapping walls
guyed down by men and kids from the town
that stayed put for a week --
sometimes on a plot of ground
that was never used for anything else
all year
The town made room for us then
welcomed us back each year
like part of themselves -- the freer
part

Back there -- then -- held
in those floppy canvas arms
there was a chance they would see
what a face can do -- the whites
of the eyes the drooping red mouth
-- even the slapping shoes --
it would all get through

All of us working together they might
laugh at themselves again   might climb
to the slippery wire
and try the impossible leap
or let go the safe swing and sail
reaching for another pair of arms!

So close I was sometimes I'd see
tears in the laughing eyes -- especially
the older ones --
and then for a moment again I'd feel as if
all the while   all of us
-- our arms around each other -- had really
been re-weaving some gigantic canvas
repairing the damaged threads
drawing in the strays

BLINDNESS

Each time there was a brief period of panic
as the struggle to see felt like a struggle to breathe
Then sudden clarity -- the reprieve --
and the forgetting

But the day it happened for good
I tumbled down and away
and felt the world recede

For a while I could still hear it --
doing business as usual --
then its muffled laughter and
its bumping shadows were gone
and it all went blank

After a while they came: dreams
of colors and flowers and faces
-- each as if it were going to stay
-- messengers without mercy
from a place lost and almost
forgotten

And then one dream   so vivid I knew
it was more than a dream
and one last dancer holding out
her hand to me
And when she was gone
all the blank had turned into

a pause -- that was waiting for me!
And I knew that my tunnel
wasn't another world at all --
it was me! -- and I was moving
turning myself inside out --
my spasms becoming one gigantic
arm reaching up and out
And I felt dizzy and excited -- full
of a memory of doing all this before:
of being born!

RELAY RACE

This morning I remember Archie
It was my sophomore high school year
And it was track
it was spike-toed track shoes and
staggered starting blocks
the 100 yd. all-out dash
it was knocked down hurdles and
sore shins and knees and no breath left
it was the 220   and the 440 and the
880yd half mile   and the never-possible mile
it was the tingling smell of liniment as
we warmed up at meets
heart pounding poised in the starting blocks
and it was taking off like a pack of hounds
at the gun
and handing off the baton

And it was Archie
Archie   famous for the 880 killer half mile race
Archie   my height   compact   lax- limbed
casual   dark crew cut worn long
Archie lounging at the starting blocks   joking
    at ease at the gun
then   almost dancing in place
as the pack moved swiftly out past him
nonchalant   as though thinking
of something else
Slow and steady keeping his place near the rear
keeping his pace for   1/4   then 1/2 the race

until you were sure he had lost it and didn't care
And then at about the 3/4 mark
a cry would go up from the crowd
just as he began slowly almost imperceptively
moving up
There he was
slow steady like a antelope finding its stride
now he passed up one now two three…

There he was perhaps 100 yards from the finish
now breaking clearly into the lead
contained gliding
first across the finish line

Now 55 years later this morning
far from
Menomonee Falls
I remember you
and I salute you Archie
like I yelled for you then

You knew your body even then
You knew your course
And you ran it your own way

A NoTE FrOM HUCK FiNn

WHOeVer geTs this here NoTe
maybee some great great grandsun of mine
hunnerd years from now
me Huck Finn your great great granddaddy
herbi want yous to now
no matter what yur daddy tells yous
that it were beter than
any kinda goode riport card
I cuda ever got
-- my advinturs with Jim
on the Misssippi

H. FINN Esq.

FROM THE DIARY OF *LE*

My name is *Le* and I wonder who I am and where
and how I came to be here with all these others and
where we are going

I awoke three passings ago
The three old wise ones who departed were *Wo*
Am and *Ih*
Ih was the most recent
Older and wiser than the others
his passing grieved everyone
He of all I have known lived up to his name:
Ih: "he who sees beneath the surface"

The day that *Ih* departed a child arrived
and was named *Ihua* :
"little one who sees beneath the surface"
Of course it was an honor
to name her this and no one thinks too much of it
She does not know where she is yet and
though she is one of us she speaks her own
language for now

She bursts in each day like a fresh wind that
reminds me of -- of what? -- another place
that I have been? Another place that I am waiting
to go to and somehow know? Another "here"
beneath the surface that she can see still and I
have become blind to?

Some are disturbed that she does not
learn more quickly
-- and there is much to be learned about our world
Our fathers and forefathers have explored
examined discussed and have written it all down
And they say "Now it is her turn to learn"
But I say, "Not so fast!"
Look! : *Ih* and *Ihua*. He with all of his years and learning
more and more seeing
beneath the surface -- seeing all we had found
and written for what it was:
          discoveries -- nothing more, nothing less
and *Ihua*, yes, grasping for every clue
but fresh in her seeing

My name is *Le* and it means "he who wonders"

PLAYING BANJO AT THE STREET FAIR
TO AN AUDIENCE OF ONE 3 YEAR OLD BOY

(for Hudson)

Your

blue-green

eyes

like worlds

empty this moment

of all

but the music

THE MYTH OF *WE -AS-A – CHILD*

Child -- do you know me?
I am the old story teller
You have seen me in the village
I seldom speak -- but when I see
a little one I know will understand
I speak to her

Take my hand…come out with me
Look at that big white moon
Sit here…listen…do you remember?

You-We began as a child awakened like this
in the night
was there a full moon? was it also the season
of lilacs?
And *We-As-A -Child* as we awoke did not see clearly
First *We-As-A-Child* breathed the whole world around us in and
stretched and reached our
small fingers and toes to touch what we could
-- mother's breast her face the smell of her skin
the feel of cloth of hair and water and fur
the smell of lilacs and grass warm sun
father's hands and the feel of his voice
-- all were like voices below whispering,
like touches on the inside -- touched *We-As-A- Child*

Then at last we saw what *We-As-A-Child* already knew from
smelling and touching and we were dazzled by seeing! -- mother's
face! father! the sky! the river! the other children!

and what we knew before seeing and what was inside our seeing
was silent and hidden in this new light
And from what we saw we made words
and wonderful stories…but we made almost no words almost no stories to remind us of what *We-As-A-Child* knew of the other deep of things
The stories that we made with our words
were missing something that *We-As-A-Child* knew

See the moon little one!
Breathe in the night air!
Remember! Do you remember?

METRO NORTH

a boy about 6

sitting

directly across

from his father

holding hands

speaking softly

EVENING OF OUTDOOR JAZZ

Only
          always
                    listen
then listen again
                              inside
  and again   inside

Listen
          for
                    one
          falling
                    first
                              raindrop
on the back of your hand

that

          changes

everything

A SEASON OF WORDS

i listened
after i spoke
after i spoke about how it felt to me
i listened to how they felt about it
i listened with more than my usual listening
i listened without excitement
without excitement about what i was going to say
suddenly dormant i submerged my saying into listening
and i watched their words fall
i watched their words fall small and crystalline on me
on me words gathered on me a heavy layer of words
words cold silencing words
and i thought "perhaps these words belong with me
are something for me that i do not want
are something perhaps that at some later time i can accept
are something perhaps i can somehow accept now for then"

and somehow then   somehow only then
only then did i begin to hear something
something not stilled by what they had said
something still liquid or just become liquid again
something left out something also belonging somehow to me
something warm and vaporous rising
something alive perhaps only in me
something alive just the same
and i spoke

RIVER

The young man leaned against his wagon
-- twilight
-- summertime
the sunset was burning the western sky

Alone --
He put more wood on the fire in front of him
sat down looking into it

Heaviness in him
lostness longing

He called to the fire and the night
for something he could not name
-- and the thought of his mother came…

She had told him once that she saw that he had
strong feelings for nature – like her

She had said,

boy, remember -- often there are no
words for what you feel in your heart
-- strong feelings for people
and life at times -- I know --
often wider and deeper than words

Son, I want you to remember something

I am going to tell you
something my grandfather told me to remember
-- you are like him too!

Always -- by a glance   a laugh   a silence
by the raising of a finger or an eyebrow
by a yell   a dance   a word…
-- always there will be a way for what is strong in you
to flow into the world -- don't hold back!
Even if you try to deny it you will never be able to for long

You are a river -- a river of warm life
even when quietly flowing   you are unbound
even when raging   overflowing   you are a gift
You are a warm river of life that must flow!
Do not despise the wildness of your flowing
Do not despair the gift of your unknown life

The young man looked into the
dancing flames

The heaviness had gone
He stood up

*

magnolia
  most voluptuous of trees

your white whisper
  finer than silk
gently completely unfolds

THE LIMP

No Mary I don't mind your asking
It's from an
accident--a long time ago
It never bothered me much
and then about three years ago it started acting up
Just some soreness at first -- then one morning
I couldn't walk at all

The doctors found an infection
then deterioration of the bone
They put me through one painful procedure after another
then therapy and finally when nothing more could be done
they gave me medication for the pain and said "Exercise!"

Just recently I've begun to realize how in one way or another that
this thing has been constantly on my mind these three years
Of course that's to be expected with something as severe as this
But it really embarrasses me now when I think of how I would haul
out my story in conversations as if it were a performing monkey --
sometimes even raising my pants' leg
like I was holding a whittled stick of wood instead of my leg!

Two weeks ago
something altogether different happened
I was taking my usual morning walk in the park struggling with each
twisted step -- and then, it was as if I had absentmindedly left it --
the limp -- somewhere behind for a whole stretch of time
because I felt it catching up with me -- tugging at my leg again!

That's happened since
I'm not losing the limp that's for sure -- but I think somehow I'm absorbing it
I think it's coming inside where it's always belonged
-- All of a sudden it's as if we've got bigger things to do together!

It was you you know   that day here in the park

COFFEE CUP

its unblinking eye
its slippery
hand its bloated tactile

brain
its dusty tongue

its
windblown
- curtained
-blue-checked- children's - years

its dusky

whitewashed room

IV

THE RIVER

*

a poem
          can be many things
puzzle of images
sweet river of sounds
knot of ideas
  but then comes
the time   sometimes
when all those things are forgotten
or perhaps they all work together
in some magical way for some someone
-- you --
and you after hearing it say
"Ah" in that special way of yours
and I feel the poem leaving the ground
taking you with it

BALZAC

(sculpture by Rodin)

At this angle
his head is higher than the mountains
behind him
his shock of hair
against the clear blue sky --
    immense
        audacious

Search for the eyes   some feature
in the form
    -- everything is inaccessible
Yet all together   in this light
        is he not breathing? -- or caught
at just the moment when
        his chest drawn up and held
his whole body is one cloaked and massive
pointing
a race of shimmering bits of silver
out of focus   drawn together
                    soaring

*

a poem is a way of loving

-- a shovel

that does real work in the world

THE RIVER

(sculpture by Aristide Malloil)

my eyes rest
on her
shoulder
slide down
to the broad flat place
at the small of her back
and
   onto her launching thigh

I will go with you

YOU WILL KNOW

So
          little one
you
          are two!
Do you know
                    how you
               are loved?
(I know you do)

All the tiny silent ways
that caring comes
          -- they rest in you
so that some day
               when you
may need it most
               brighter than the sun
          at noon
you will know
     how we love you

PROMETHEUS

You broke through
at dusk
striding east
flying your own huge shadow
in the bed of the sun

Perhaps you knew
I would not hold my darkness dear
or weave from my accustomed gloom
some garment or a velvet glove
but stretch out my hand
link bone with bone
lay hold upon -- not only the flickering light --
but the clandestine scent
of the flame

SNOW WALK

standing alone on woods road
drifts of untouched snow
under the trees

the last car disappears

soundless
   closing of a temple door

*

poem written on the back

of a parking stub

-- empty jar that fills the hand

ODYSSEUS--TO HIS DAUGHTER
(for Shannon)

"My father stood before me and placed the
helmet on my head, the armor on my shoulders, and
the shield in my hands
And at my side he hung the
sword of his father

"Then he turned   facing the sea on the high windy hill
and he said:

'This house and this garden are too small
for you now
Haven't you already been awakened at dawn
by the whispering touch of Pallas Athena --
haven't I seen you looking with longing at the
casting-off ships?

'It is time to place all of your belongings into
a small bag and to join with comrades
hoisting the sail
It is time to lend your hand to a large destiny:
to see the impossible ranged in front of you
in one of a thousand faces
calling all the possible in you to life
-- to steer alone and trembling through
heavy darkness and to land on strange forbidding
shores, even the shores of Hades
and to bear even the wrath of Zeus

'To find yourself awakening on a hillside
beside a strange sea
with the ship of Athena waiting and the benevolent
winds of inscrutable Zeus billowing the sails
and the sun -- your own sun rising --
and the earth -- your own earth   your own ground
beneath your heavy sandaled feet
and the clasp of tested friends
and the home you have been given and have
won back'

"Then he embraced me and I him   and I left

"And now   my daughter   my love
          here is the helmet and the armor
          here is the shield   and the sword"

*

This emptiness
is filling me
and I am slipping
into my life

like a hand into its glove
like autumn into the world

THIS HAWK

This hawk
has only known the cage
-- leather strap around his leg
he knows hunger though
one hunger
    blood filled
-- to the bone he knows it

so when the man
slipped off the strap
to replace it
    he struck
                he gouged
       he ripped
he tore
  he lunged
     he hopped
he grasped his way to
the top of this tree

His eyes are red
          and wild
he shakes
he blinks at the descending sun
his smallest feathers are ruffling
in the wind
He hardly knows his body
and it must save him now

Only
his breath is
soaring
pulsing
all the way
to his wing-tips
again again
now the quivering
the quick slight strokes
now the heavy
savage
beating the air
the leaden body casting off
the splayed wings
pumping like oars

the buoyant resonant air

the

high

shrill

cry

JUST BEFORE

Just before dawn
when night still holds sway
over everything
          except a slight band of sandy haze
   that gives way to powder blue
just above the hills

And the quarter moon
bathes my hands like a candle
as I sit before my open door
          bats whirling among the chimneys
  house wren's song streaming the silence

Dawn   dreams
    -- dew of the still-possible
gathers on the yet-not-day

YES AND NO

"You must change your life"—Rilke

In the matter of changing your life
I now believe it is not a question
of finding out
how

The river pushes harder
  against the banks as it
deepens
    pushes to overflow
spills into new
      folds among the tall weedy
reeds
splashes against the rocks and
  falls into new forms
It is full it is bursting
like fruit

And the pressure of this fullness
in you
requires of you now
the collaborative
  yes
that opens the outer doors

In the time of ripeness
          all else is no

*

(for Tana)

Late afternoon
my   writing   stops

-- daughter

talking to her train

*

Jacaranda
purple and green against
blue
scattering full blossoms
onto the road

This letting go
is flooding the air
with faces that I love

*

just outside
our dining room window
-- a blooming red tulip tree

you
in the middle of the floor
twirling your small heart out

RED

Red
the yarn for
  Annie's hair

One package is already
on her child-made head
that rises so triumphantly
above the fragile chest
the painted heart the dangling
    legs

Off you go
cradled in the arms
of your small god
(creation out of cloth and thread
-- you leave them far behind)

TRANSFORMATION
(for Cale and Anika)

Throughout your slow obscure lunge
toward light
your learning was intuitive
touching obstacles unseen

And now
your small hearts pulsing
you whirl in light and air
your stems and leaves
unraveling
night and moisture in another form

HOUSE OF WHISPERS HOUSE OF SKINS

A house for what is missing
          here someone has been building
          but not conventionally
          here someone has made an altar for
          the air
                        of skins
          here someone has woven skins
          into an open lattice
             a basket for holding
            what no one can see

Who loves the wind
          and rain and sun and
          falling snow on their head
      will love this home
leaves will float down into their
          soup
birds and squirrels will wander in
freely and gather up
crumbs

A sacred thing to be a home for
          what has no home
no furniture to make things sit still
no solid walls or roof to
roof things out
no doors or locks
everything is welcome here
   and on its own terms

What might come here
of mine
out of lacking a home with me?
what if I listen to the whisper of that
…follow that whisper of mine
here
and myself lie
quietly
nearby
so as not to frighten it
simply let it breathe
beneath these stars

V

AFTER RAIN

IN SPRING

in spring too   there is death
    death of the cloistered seed-life
the open tomb and
unsteady legs that must support
strange passages
disarrayed senses that will try to hold
the piquant scent in the rubric of
the old

in spring too   there is pain
    the ancient tree is unnerved
again
    and all things quiver
in the hand of life

SUMMER RAIN

(for P.B.)

Follow the heavy scent
to Michigan summers   warm rain
and graves and flowers on graves and
the huge web of primal stillness
pricked by the single sound of a high
hidden crow in the court of the oaks

go down   go through and
down drenched footpaths
where the blossoms   clotted and brown
are catching the slow splashing drops
from the leaves

go down in time with
the warm rain   go through and down
to the wound in time
to the cry
ripping the ground   to the hot gasps
between cries gathering cries
beating the air

go through   go through and down
time   through the wound in time
there
-- through the window
-- off in the distance!
look -- through the bushes -- just over the wall

sauntering
secure
peopling the air

THE CRY

Here no one could see or hear him

He slumped to his knees in the tall grass
        his elbows pressed against his waist
his knuckles dug into the ground
        and he rocked forward
        then swung back
        and his open mouth stretched up
        and wide
        his fingers splayed
        his elbows thrust into his stomach
and the floor of his belly
        swelled at his throat
              again and   again
until there
        at his throat
        his whole body burst fury and fire
lava and thunder
from the center of the world
to whatever else there was

AFTER RAIN

Thousands of mirrors
  sparkling the trees
wet streets   and wind
  in the chimes

Whispers in darkness
  waves of light
and a boat   on the porch
  full of flowers

THE MOST BEAUTIFUL DAY OF THE YEAR

The most beautiful day of the year
Three children have been shot in Pasadena
Red liquidambar leaf hands everywhere curling clutching
life
Chalk scrawls on the sidewalk circles swirls names
Three children shot in Pasadena
Standing in brilliant
sunshine
Walking beneath the tree fort built of planks
Three children shot in Pasadena
Bougainvillea bursting with red
Three children
Scent of pine
Three children
Shining eucalyptus
Three children
The most beautiful day of the year
Shot.

WINTERGARDEN

the sad gate swings

            -- wet stones

unswept bouquets

AFTER VISITING MY MOTHER IN A CONVALESCENT HOSPITAL

Some structure I have worked so hard
to build and occupy
now is clearly rusting away
In this half light I remember
desolate corridors
and I see faces again like stars
I remember the pitch blackness
of strange rooms
and I hear voices like warm winds
There is a hand again like the sun

The land is reasserting itself in me
Something is coming home
about just being here
about having my heart broken
open
scattered like seed
on the hungering wind

*

Leave room for fear
better
        to wonder why it comes
better
        to see it trembling at the heel of joy
    and kneeling down
    feel some new courage
        rise

EPIPHANY

My magi
were my poems
long slow travelers
      great rhythms of longing
that finally broke
   broke me
    brought me plunging
   piece-meal
to this ground I never would have reached
in any other way
flung me through fire into this form
I never could have chosen:
   bones
     lapped and crossed lying shoulder to
      shoulder and reaching
   the fragile uprights and the wan column
like
   some strange aboriginal assortment of sticks
    and stone
a marker for other travelers
        a human trace

We are the knob
and together the turning
we are the trembling together
on the wind of an open door

FOR A FRIEND WHOSE SON DIED YOUNG

(for J.P.)

Languid scarecrow
head drooping
the birds are tugging
at your hands and your hair
the wind is dancing
with your arms
all the simple connections are
trying

Love the one great intuition
immense with sadness and joy
is taking you in

"JUST LIKE PHIL"

(for my father)

It was a curse that
-- with his temper and all --
we used to fling at one another
when he wasn't there
Of course he mellowed but it seemed his epitaph

Now that mouth is still
his eyes are quiet
yet thinking back
they mostly always were
-- part of a silence I could not comprehend then
and no one talked about

As time went on
more and more he looked you steady
in the face
and stars and hummingbirds
and maple trees and death
with a silence like a quiet hand on the shoulder
you knew was there

And then one day after he was gone
Upset -- I called my sister Judy
and from 2000 miles away I heard "I know…I know"
just like Phil

*

you see
this present moment
is an incredible wilderness
in which
I simply do the best I can

SAD AND GENTLE GIANT

(for Eric Garner)

Look at his eyes
his face
hear his voice:

"Officers, I'm not doing anything
wrong
Just leave me alone!"
pleading
Watch his arms
unthreatening
like a flailing child
trying to clear a space of safety
trying to clear space to breathe

Prolong this moment
Stand for this moment
with him
hear his tears of anger
and fear
a man alone
desperate for help

Stand with him
Watch the pack slowly circle
draw in

Stand with him
Be the cop on the beat

who wasn't there
who comes up just then
and says
"Hey Eric -- what's going down man?"
who
puts his hand on his shoulder
and says
"Hold everything....tell me, man.
It'll be ok...Tell me!"

PRESIDENTIAL ELECTION 2016 (2 poems)

A "VICTORY"

He flung out
a wide net
of hatred
hatred worked for him
-- gathered in these disaffected

He had no plan
but with his visceral snarl
he provoked theirs until it seethed

IN THESE TIMES

When you begin
to cringe   to turn towards denial
to hide
Pause a moment
look into the eyes
-- hold the terrified one
Breathe
your full presence
Embody your ground

JOHN BROWN'S FARM

snow sweeps past his bronze head
and on down
            the farm's wide lane

the place is quiet now
as of a life found
            -- gone deep

NET OF TEARS

One said
        "We're free!
We declare our freedom as a people!
We demand our homeland's place in the circle of nations!
And you -- we will not be threatened by you into silence!
We will not bargain to live here free of you!
We declare what can never be bargained:
        We're free!

"We're giddy   we're drunk with the wind from the high hills
                -- Don't you feel it?
Your settlements on our land
Your troops in our cities
Your blockades of our ports   are useless now
                -- Don't you see it?
This land of sand and blood cries out
        "Enough!"-- don't you hear it?
Ah! -- We're breaking this net of tears!
                We're free!

"Two nations--make no mistake in what we say!
                Two nations! -- you and us
-- we begin with our freedom!
In freedom can we bargain
    -- peace if we can have it!
No guarantees -- but this chance -- don't you feel it?
                We're free!"

**

The other said
"Stop!
What is the meaning of this shouting of
your freedom to the world?
Freedom from what? From us?
First you must negotiate with us
for this land!
First you must negotiate with us
for peace and security!
When we hear you shouting your name and
your freedom to the world
our hearts tremble
for this land for our lives!

"Ah! This land of blood and sand!
You will not say from your hearts that we had
a terrible right to come here!
You will not say from your hearts that we had
a terrible right to do what we did!
You will not say from your hearts that we have
a right to be here!

"Ah! this net of tears!
Your presence oppresses our hearts!
Your freedom threatens our home!
We can not bear to look you in the face
and we can not let you go!"

REDUCED TO STONE

(Three poems)

REDUCED TO STONE:

WHEN IN THE COURSE OF HUMAN EVENTS

He was a taxi driver in the small village of Yakubi
  in Afghanistan
  his name was
    Dilawar
"**All men are created equal**...."

He had a wife and a child
    Dilawar
"**They are endowed by their Creator**...."

One day he was stopped by an Afghan warlord
Turned over to the US military
Terrified
He never had a hearing
Terrified
Evidence was never presented against him
Terrified
    Dilawar
"**With certain unalienable rights**...."

He was brought to the United States Military prison at Bagram
Terrified
He was placed in isolation
Terrified
He was deprived of sleep
Terrified

After a short while it was obvious to his interrogators
that he had no information to give
Terrified
    Dilawar
"That among these are
Life, liberty, and the pursuit of happiness..."

His US government guards hung him by his wrists in isolation
Brutalized
He screamed
Terrified
They kicked him
Brutalized
He called out to God
Terrified
No one stopped them
Brutalized
Over and over they kicked his legs
Brutalized
Until his body was pulverized
Brutalized
    Dilawar
"**that to secure these rights, governments...**"

He was deprived of sleep
Brutalized
He was hallucinating
Brutalized
They told him to shut up
Brutalized
He kept screaming

Brutalized
He was yanked from his cell
Brutalized
Shackled he was beaten
Brutalized
He was hung in isolation and kicked over and over
Brutalized
No one stopped them
In the United States of America prison in Bagram
Dilawar
“**that to secure these rights, governments**...”

There were no Geneva Conventions to protect him
Brutalized
In the United States prison in Bagram
Dilawar
“**that to secure these rights, governments**...”

There was no UN Convention Against Torture
To protect him
Brutalized
In the United States prison in Bagram
Dilawar
“**that to secure these rights, governments**...”

There was no Habeas Corpus
To protect him
Brutalized
In the United States prison in Bagram
Dilawar
“**that to secure these rights, governments**...”

No one stopped them
The orders from above were "take the gloves off"
In the United States of America prison in Bagram
Terrified
He had nothing but his name
Dilawar
"**that to secure these rights, governments**..."

No one stopped them
Terrified
After while they kicked him
Brutalized
just to hear him scream
they said
Terrified
Dilawar
"**that to secure these rights, governments**..."

The military coroner's report
No one stopped them
Said "the cause of his death was"
No one stopped them in the United States of America
Prison in Bagram
"homicide"
No one stopped them in the United States of America
Dilawar
"**that to secure these rights, governments**..."

No one stopped them
No one
Dilawar

REDUCED TO STONE:

CALL IT BY ANY NAME

[***The <u>United Nations Convention Against Torture</u>*** *came into force on April 18, 1988. The United States signed and ratified it Oct.21, 1994 investing it with full legal authority.]*

We knew what they were driving at
Or was it rather that *they* knew what we would be driven *toward*
now post 9/11 in wits-end-war and so
they said
  No severe pain and suffering may be inflicted on a person
  for the purpose of obtaining information...
they said
  No one may be subjected to torture or to cruel, inhuman
  or degrading treatment...
they said
  There are no exceptional circumstances

We knew what they meant

We drove ourselves ahead or were driven
frothing at the mouth
" Information! We have to have it! What they did to us!
  What they might still do!"
We weighed suffering and cruelty in permissible degrees
against our demand for "information" -- lead-heavy
  with fear
So when the detainees didn't hand over the goods
we stepped up the program by god

It was almost impossible to tell the good prospects
from the bad -- sometimes we really didn't care
and just beat them like
Dilawar in Bagram
until they died or spoke
gibberish

There is a screaming in our ears that logic will not drown
We wish to be done with all that now
but is our fear done riding us?
Our President says
we will use the Army Field Manual
with our detainees now
If so
  sleep deprivation
  prolonged isolation
  the "psychological healing arts" will break them
and we will call what we do
by another name

Some of us are sick
We need to find another way

They said
    No one may be subjected to cruel treatment…
Now we can add the words we know they meant for us:
   Call it by any name -- do no cruelty -- not for any purpose.
   You will be convinced that
    you have exceptional circumstances
     -- you do not
   Beware the blood-red eye of wild- fear

Beware   crazed-information–mania
blinding-vindictiveness
-- they will come
We know these paths

Now their words are not naive to us
They who knew war-fear and guilt and horror at least as much
as we were warning us
pointing us toward something
elemental
that we would have to find ourselves was true

REDUCED TO STONE:

A MEDITATION

1

Here
the
terrifying one
and
I
were once
both

reduced to
stone

2

Move

slowly

through these

fields

pause

somehow...

kneel down

and touch your feet

now

for then

stretch out your arms

and breathe

3

this

stillness absolute:

my

presence

*

Like some blind fruit
pressing up against
its inner wall
I feel
across the boundary
the trembling
of another wind
the ripening of another sun

FOR EDWARD

you died
yesterday
            hit by a bus
    riding your bike

-- your stillness
     falls   on
                everything

I am waiting
         over time
weaving
all I can
in the basket of my hands

THIS KNOWLEDGE

This is the knowledge that lies right
below the surface in me and yet eludes me
This is the knowledge that I see precedes
all knowledge in me this is the silent knowledge
that I see precedes all words

This is the knowledge that lay like a seed
in me not yet opened when the world opened
to me
This is the knowledge that opened and
that continues to open me
the gift that continues to open my life:
This is the knowledge in me of
your dignity my brother my sister
whoever you are

This knowledge deserves a better name
I call it *bliss*
This knowledge rising in me
kernel of bliss
scent of wholeness
joy in my bones
This is the primal knowing I have
of your preciousness my brother my
sister to me
that
I know suddenly
like a lightning bolt in my darkness

that I know in some shadowy part of myself
like a soft light half-hidden glowing
that I know in the presence of confusion and fear
in the shock of awakening
and in sadness remembering
and in hope rising

This I know
like a scent that I love again
and can not give up loving

Something missing in me
you call into being
something for both of us
something unheard of before
something beyond what this place
praises or denies

You
my brother my sister whoever you are
you are transforming fire

VI

SHARECROPPING

*

I move in music
that no one can hear

my words
are fragments
of a song in me
beneath
    all songs

HUNTINGTON LIBRARY: BESIDE THE POND

half asleep lying beside a bush
bird call
-- so close
I am
the streaming fluid
the brazen rasp
in his throat

**

Cool wind
at my waist
-- across suddenly bare skin

This liquid moment

ALLEY WALK

The gate to the meditation garden is
          locked at St. Luke's so I sit
on a
          curbstone

In there St. Francis holds a bird
                    in his broken hand
          and water drips and trickles down
the rusty brown fountain and a padlock
now keeps out loiterers like me

The alley on the other hand is always here
          so I walk toward home with a view
   of the backs of the houses

the white house   its garage   tilting and
          white paint blistering in a thousand tiny rectangles

an old plastic soda bottle and a chest without drawers lining the
narrow asphalt alley-way   a row of weeds firmly entrenched in
the center
off to the side a discarded sofa
          its styrofoam ripped to shreds
blue morning glories roaming
            over the wall up the
telephone pole

broken green glass   pink confetti

an empty car-port its dark oil-spotted concrete swept clean
a summer job poster with rip out telephone numbers
a   slat fence   sagging
blue stucco garage

At the end   the mortuary
its red oleander   its vegetable garden and
Ed spraying his corn

We talk corn as we have before
but this time about how you watch the color of the
tassels to see when they're brown
I tell him I'd like to buy a couple from him when they're ready
and he disappears down a small row
then returns and
stands there in his straw hat
his hand extended   kind of like St. Francis
except he has no love for birds
and he tosses me an ear

LAUNCH

The way the
gull shrieks
    -- hangs in the wind
right in front of my face
above the jumble of rocks
at the edge of the river

then casts her lead gray body
off before me
pumping her heavy wings
like oars

The way
my shoulder blades
almost quiver
with expectation
all the walk home

SHARECROPPING

He didn't bother
pulling out the sunflowers
so two lie along the fence
slowly drying
and one
stands upright
at the back of the small barren plot
-- a brown shaggy figure
in its rags
and wide dry hat-head hanging

One day last summer
he was there working the garden
as I walked by on my way home
I stopped
We talked
He said he rented the land
from the surrounding mortuary
just grew enough for himself
and his friends

Standing in front of the rows of corn
with lettuce and squash
blooming at his feet
he offered me a gigantic sunflower
bulging with seeds
and said
"don't roast them --
eat them like the birds"

Now
a jagged walkway of warped
boards lies on the dusty ground
A white plastic bucket
            sits
       still upside down
          (I saw him sitting on it once
               mid-July
               large hat drooping -- asleep)
at the end of one of the short dried rows of stubble

A net of useless strings
swings lightly in place between tall stakes
Hoe
         rake   spade
lean against the garage

STANDING FIGURE--THE KNIFE EDGE

(sculpture by Henry Moore)

The view from the front will tell you nothing
even the head is not a landmark
in this sea
For once see things as they are -- unexpected
the random patches of stripped
and pebbled flesh
the singing ridge of thinly covered
bone -- the rib   like the cutting edge
of a wing
like the bow of a running ship
the two surfaces flying
smoothly away
the weathered leg
like a rudder -- holding true

the powerful protective curving of the back
billowing high at the shoulders
urging you up
like a small flag
to boil in the wind

COMMUNION

(for C.B.)

In the midst of the season which humiliates
    and burns
during the reign
of the wound which will not heal
under the revolving wheel of hatred and
        despair

For you
    who feel the immense obstacle in the dark
    unable to gauge its height
    its terrible silent size
whose head must lie on a fingerless
        flat hand

For you dark sailor
        and for me
  out of the cry billowing tight in our throats
  out of our fingers stretched taut to the limit
the darkness between us quivering
    like some great wing

*

the
hawk

soars into silence

on her wingtips

she glides
into her body

COLD WALK

20 degrees this morning
scarf around my mouth
artic-flap hat
down jacket mittens
hiking boots

Puffing I take it slow...muttering a bit
when the hooded and wrapped shadow
on my right
informs me that I am moving like an
alert trappper in winter
so slow that now
I can see
how the thin trunks of bushes emerge from the
snow over there
so slow that now I can see individual thorns on
these tiny branches
so slow that looking at my shadow again
I seem peering...
acquainting myself
with whatever drifts into view
as though I have shifted (just by walking slow enough)
into becoming some scrooge-like neighbor
suddenly excitedly amazingly
on friendly terms with everyone and
everything
"Hello there! And a good day to you!"

So slow
that I seem to have caught the
rhythm of these whereabouts
and am meandering among them
somehow in sync
   like that jazz combo I just heard
who have played
together so many years you can hardly
distinguish the different instruments'
sounds...so blending...
            like that
so slow that some music   some blend of presences
some new exchange
is taking place here with me

The doe's tracks in the snow
now   are today's   yesterday's
            those of 40 years ago
all at once

ALBA PLENA

Under this branch-tangled dome
            of live-oaks
thousands of camellias bloom
The reds are dying now
but this bush is alive with white
And one blossom
              eye level
                     sings out so loudly
that I search for its name:
           "Alba Plena"

So perfectly formed
                     white on white on white
                     interrupted layer by layer
only by hints of yellow shadow
deep toward the center

There behind you rides the sun
There is no scent from you but that of cold silk
no sound but your name

The path is shadow on shadow ahead
except for one pool of light
Stopping there   turning
   -- a dazzling river of light
           is pouring through the wispy translucent grass
              flowing over and around a black half-buried trunk
    spraying chaotic strands of spider web   particles of dust   gnats
splashing off the hard small backs

of the myriad live-oak leaves at my feet

All around shadows hover
The darkness here is not dangerous

*

scattered
in sun
a sun
on each

slender

stalk

mother of a thousand
breaths
of delight

S
K
Y

SAILOR

my boat
smooth eucalyptus
bleached

hung
r
y
m
u u w
c l s e
for u a
v s

& e nd le ss bl u e

FLYING BRIDGE

She thought she saw in some mist
    half hidden

    a bridge
severed from the land
    -- “flying”
connecting what seemed impossible
    in one part of her self
        with another
connecting what seemed impossible
    between her
      and the others

And she was filled with longing
    and fear   and joy

(after a poem by Chinese poet Zhang Xu 670 ? CE
entitled “Peach Blossom Spring”)

CICADAS IN THE MORNING CICADAS IN THE EVENING

Walking into town
drone of the cicadas
        answered by the roar
of leaf-blowers

The cicadas have my vote

Imagine each one
adding to the chorus
    -- the resonance they must feel
in their plump and tuned red-eyed bodies
"Alive! Alive! Alive! I'm here too !"

(as if they needed words
                to make it true)

TWO CHINESE POEMS:

IN THE GREEN MOUNTAINS

You ask me why
I make my home
in the green mountains

I smile
and do not speak
my heart is at rest

Peach blossoms
are drifting with the river
the world goes deep
beyond all we know

-- Li Bai (Chinese 701-762 CE)
(trans. Jim Glaser)

DAO DE JING #40

The deepest moves by returning
  and it works through gentleness

Regardless of how things seems
  a deep emptiness
brings all things to life

-- Laozi (Chinese 600 ? BCE)
(trans. Jim Glaser)

SAILING OFF REDONDO BEACH

Here no speech intrudes
on the rise and fall of primal sighs
    and the wide maternal hand
        caressing the shore
beckons again and again

Here even the wind is blue
        and the smooth underbelly
          of my life glides naively
on unsounded depths

You signal your coming
        with a flutter of ribbons
and the rigging rings
The skiff is a quiver of canvas
racing shoulder to shoulder
and free
  -- suddenly too fast
                too far off balance
-- I swing directly into the wind

Catching my breath
                I go on
following the shore
stretching the line of my present life
by degrees

drawn by a taste of salt

VII

BLUE

A NOTE TO ODYSSEUS

(for B.G. B.W. N.F. J.C.)

I write this to you from my new
home
  It is dark now
The water is dark and unruffled
The house is large and old
A new home
  yet enough like the
other for me to hear old voices
And on some nights to awaken trembling

And there are deep friendly
voices here
The voices of friends like you
And deep in my bones your voice

The passage was rough and long and we had to
be perfectly still through part of it
And part of it we slept in shifts
  with our arms around each other
We helped one another keep still
We helped one another keep faith
We faced
We went through
We are here

Feel my hand reaching back
  to clasp yours

*

walk before dawn

-- fine drizzle
against my lips

*

The
wind
has blown away the heavy world
that occupied me yesterday

leaving
you
sharp and clear
full
of mystery

THE STRANGER

He spoke a new language
that made no sense
at first
but the sounds
reminded you of other things

and I wondered if maybe
that was what he was trying
to communicate: what we were
reminded of

It was as if
knowing that the secret places
he had found were his alone
he still had to try
to touch them
with his tongue

SWEET CLOVER

wind
blown

this luscious
embodiment

I have always wanted

this love
my
breathing body knows

*

spring
-- light rain

I drift in scent

*

a stillness
          comes

things are right
   for the first time
… as if for the first time

and you are here

   as if for the first time

*

There never was
more than a path
just a trace of brown
beneath the yellow grass
but it was enough

and my hands were free
to cradle the leaves
for a moment
just as they fell

WITH LOVE

Its premature arrival
its unlikely habitat
its omnivorous heady shade
its slow excruciating seeds

Its adoptive wink
its earthbound thigh
its reedy skin
its windblown orphaned hair

Its transfusing breath its petaled cheek
its salty chin
its bubbling
star strung smile

its riddled pace
its ambiguous steady feet

*

morning after rain

-- my body

a net for the wind

*

(for Naaz)

presence is a country

--face of the moon

thin slippered feet

on a wooden floor

I HAVE COME

I have come
        from my troubles
to this place of
        wild winds
this raucous
        festival of leaves

you
    your hair pulled back
                on either side
        flamboyant skirts
flying
       -- you are the queen

DAWN GIRL

Dawn girl
beside me on the lawn
raising your head

Your wind blown hair
your emerald eyes

looking down at me

*

morning
            you walk by
in your white robe

-- deeper
          than words

I SEEM TO HEAR SMALL BELLS
(2 poems for Beth and Hugh)

I seem to hear small bells
and become quite still
stillness breathes in me
the silence of things rises
sweet and far
I seem to hear small bells

**

Today
again
the doors open
the doors to the world
open to you

Love opens the doors
once again love
opens
the doors of life
for you

Love inherent in you
-- go through
love showered on you
-- go through the doors

*

Lying
holding each other
your body and mine folded together
I felt love
huge and yet in us
come natural as breath

turning things upside down

BLUE

You
my sensible eye
so preoccupied with sky
and snow and   people with dogs
and trains and parks
and rooftops and smoke
and all that frightens and
blazes   sings and laughs
-- Do you not notice
my other musing
yet hungry   eye
opening   closing
more   rapidly now
streams of sturdy hope
invading my senses
winds of freedom
filling my nostrils
my whole body drawing together

diving
into the unknown

one blue wave

CASCADING TIME

(Poems on titled paintings by Diane Churchill)

"*Cascade*"

you gather and release
so effort–less
I love your folds

… what is the secret of your release?

"*Touch*"

liquid threads streaming through
my fingers
long black longing
arc

aura of the slightest yellow
drawing me
here
where you
lean
impossiby
against
light pink

here -- where nothing is expected

to

happen!

Right here!

"EROS"

You wider
than names
wider
un-named in me
My unknown body opens
life-drenched
in joy

You quiver the scarecrow
-- he flies from the pole
Here he comes!
dancing the leaves
waving the sky

Look how he shines!

ON THE WAY

On the way
I had nightmares
On the way
in panic
I abandoned myself

On the way
I reached down
and gathered myself
in my huge arms
and strode out
to where you
kneeling
were tending your flowers

Your eyes met mine
no words
then some words
no touch
then the brushing of our hands

The lightest kiss I have ever known

ALL THE WORDS

All the words
including these
miss the mark
and still we meet

Beneath beyond all words
and through all words through everything
you flow
meandering swirling
leaping
wild and not so wild
you flow persistently
to me

You paint and I hear singing
you breathe blue
my windows open
your touch
cascades my nakedness
my fingers tremble over your belly
I shiver
in the ocean of your eyes
and babble my native clicking tongue
You speak with swallows eyes
and flamenco feet
We fly
the desert's rose-tented sky
the windy island's palms the jagged mountain ridge

arm in arm
we leap and shriek with all the others
in the turquoise whomping surf
We lose
and find each other's lips
again   again
thigh to thigh
we lie
beneath the caravan of clouds
we dive
in the honey of
moonlight
into
the silent jasmine's heart

SILHOUETTE

Tonight the wind
whirling nursemaid to the
tiny leaves
gathered them in the center
of the road
and whisked them home
and all the trees and houses
laid aside their separateness
and waved
and watched them go